Why SUPERSTAR SALES PROFESSIONALS HAVE NO COMPETITION

About **Rome**

Rome Madison is an author and expert on innovation. His consulting firm, The Superstar Academy, works with medical sales organizations to identify patterns of complacency that gradually result in loss of revenue and market share, and applies strategies to build a culture that promotes competition and sales excellence.

Rome is a former SVP and life science industry pioneer who launched two the most successful genomic sales companies in the world. He recruited and led superstar sales professionals to build elite sales and marketing teams that became the foundation of the precision medicine industry.

Drawing from life experiences with his mentally ill mother who battled homelessness, a failed pro football career, and unlikely journey from unemployed to becoming a genomic sales expert, Rome delivers principles to rethink how we approach our work, to breakthrough overwhelming barriers, and forge an innovative team culture that builds industry-leading companies.

ROME INSPIRED US BUT ALSO TOUCHED OUR HEARTS
- Clifton Johnson, Comerica Bank Empower Series

ROME GAVE ONE OF THE BEST LIVING UNITED SPEECHES I'VE EVER HEARD
- David Corteras, Executive Director
United Way of Grayson Co

ROME IS AN AMAZING SPEAKER! HE ENERGIZED THE AUDIENCE
- Jeff Klein, Meeting Planner

ROME IS DYNAMIC AND ENGAGING WITH A DELIVERY THAT WARRANTS ACTION! HE CAN ADD VALUE TO YOUR ORGANIZATION ON EVERY LEVEL. I ENJOYED THE RELATIVE CONTENT AND THE CHALLENGE TO BE BETTER IN MY PERSONAL AND PROFESSIONAL LIFE
- Aaron Davis, President
DFW National Sales Network

To Kimmie, Marloh and Zoi.

You keep me motivated to learn more, grow more and SELL MORE!!

Introduction

I'll never forget my very first national sales meeting!

It was the annual meeting where the top reps in the company were to be recognized as Superstars or Rising Stars. The top 10-20%.

I had only been with the company for six months, but I was eager to meet the people whose names would be called during the awards ceremony. As a highly competitive former college athlete I was very interested in finding out why these reps were the best and what made them different from everyone else in the company.

More importantly, I wanted to see how I measured up to these sales superstars. Were they hard charging and high energy like many of the competitors I knew from sports? Did they exude charisma and charm that made them irresistible? Did they look like cross-fit models that starred in toothpaste commercials on the weekends?

I must admit, I had these preconceived notions in my head, and there were plenty of sales people in the company that fit the description. However, during the awards ceremony when the top sales professionals were revealed, it blew my mind that the top two performers were nothing like I had imagined.

I realized that I sat by one of them earlier in the general session. She didn't say much in the meeting, and she mentioned by the end of the day that it was getting close to her bedtime and wasn't excited about staying up late for the awards banquet. After taking pictures with the other award winners, she was out of there!

The other top sales performer was very social, but compared to many of the sales people in the company, his personality....in a word, was awkward. In a group of energetic sales professionals partying after an awards banquet, he was reserved and somewhat serious. He was a nice guy, and would certainly speak to anyone who spoke to him, but he was nowhere close to being the most charismatic guy in the room.

Have you ever made an assumption about someone prior to meeting them, only to find out you were totally wrong? If so, you're certainly not alone. Studies have demonstrated that the majority of the population pass judgment on someone's ability to be successful based on appearances.

My hope is this book not only changes how you look at sales people and evaluate talent, but that it also changes how you see yourself as a sales professional.

This happened for me at my first company sales meeting.

I discovered these two award winners, who were nothing like I expected, were Superstar Sales Professionals in the truest sense because they had absolutely no competition!

They had won the top sales awards in the company for the last four years, and before then while each was in a different division of the company, they were the top sales performers in their respective divisions.

My theory of superstar looks and magnetism equating to success in selling was blown out of the water. And fortunately that compelled me to move beyond superficial thinking to recognize the true qualities that elite sales professionals in different companies and industries share in common.

I've come to realize that all sales professionals have superstar potential, but few are willing to put forth the effort and discipline to achieve that level of success.

According to The Harvard Business Review, on average 60% of salespeople in any given organization meet or exceed their sales quota of revenue goals each year. However, Superstar Sales Professionals hold themselves to a higher standard and are in a class all their own.

From my experience in sales leadership I've observed three distinct groups of sales professionals:

- **The Mid-Level Sales Performer:** the bar of performance tends to hover around 80% and below for this group. In healthy organizations they tend to be the bottom third of sales professionals, but without effective coaching and leadership vision, this group can easily swell.

  While some companies turnover the bottom 10% each year, others keep these employees because they would rather maintain continuity in the team and in the territory with hopes of improvement rather than create disruption. They are not useless; they simply lack proper motivation and skill to be an elite sales performer.

- **The Solid Sales Performer:** this group is what every sales manger hopes to find when hiring a candidate. They consistently achieve 85-100% of sales goals each year, and are often promoted into leadership positions in the organization. What I often see with this group is the yo-yo effect in sales performance from year-to-year: one year up, next year down. One year a sales award winner, the next year is spent struggling to achieve an increased and challenging quota. The solid sales performer is indeed talented, but does not have the discipline or habits that makes a superstar sales pro.

- **The Superstar Sales Professional:** this elite group of sales professionals are the reps who are in the top 10% of the stack rankings year in, and year out. They have no real competition other than their own goals and expectations. They often resist or turn down opportunities for advancement because it is not uncommon for them to earn more than their managers, and in some cases they are the highest paid employees in the company. Not because they are more talented or know more than their peers. They are elite because they maintain a daily mindset and disciplined habits that enable them to instinctually apply a high level of skill in every sales conversation.

  Which group are you in?

  LET ME BE CLEAR.....there is nothing wrong with being in any of these categories!! (unless you're in danger of losing your job!)

My definition of success is: the constant achievement of one's goals and dreams. If you are happy with your quality of life and find fulfillment through the pursuit of your own goals, that is what matters most in life.

I'm writing this book to demystify what takes to be an elite sales performer. Besides the numbers, you are closer to being a superstar than you may think.

They are not otherworldly. They are not blessed with gifts or talents that make them destined for success in sales.

The Superstar Sales Professional, famous entertainers, world-class athletes and other people who are considered the best in the world at what they do, all share a common quality that makes them elite:

SKILL

Elite sales professionals are simply the most practiced and the most disciplined professionals. It is less about inherent gifts or abilities that make them special; instead, it is their commitment and uncommon drive to develop **skills and habits** that distinguish themselves from all other sales professionals.

I am not writing this to pressure you into believing you need to be a Superstar Sales Pro.

However, when I started my sales career I was a mid-level performer and didn't know it. And every since that first sales meeting when I realized looks and a great personality don't guarantee success in sales, I've been on a quest to find what makes a sales person a superstar performer.

Since that time through self-awareness I grew into a Solid Sales Performer and achieved Superstar status as an individual contributor. More importantly, I've had the honor of coaching and mentoring sales people to be solid performers, and observing what they did to become Superstar Sales Pros.

I have come to realize there are only two things you can control in sales:

1. What you know.

2. What you do.

The purpose of this book is to give you 20+ years of truths I've observed that distinguish Superstar Sales Pros from everyone else.

What you do with this information is up to you.

Star Power is your inner ability you have to create more of what you want……by using more of what you already have.

Why
Superstar Sales Proffesionals
Have no
Competition

54 Skills and Habits of Elite Sales People

1. Ask Great Questions

This is the hallmark of the superstar sales pro! In any communal situation, the person who asks a thought-pro-voking, well-timed question can control a conversation without saying much. **Salespeople who ask great questions stand out in the customer's mind.** And they make selling look easy in the eyes of their peers. Because superstars make a habit out of using this skill, they never experience moments of uncomfortable silence in sales conversations. And they learn more about their customers' business and personal life by building trusting relationships faster than other sales pros. Great questions reveal facts and percep-tions that a customer wouldn't otherwise admit - giving you more information to close early and often.

Salespeople are the ultimate problem solvers. The best way to solve a potential customer's problem is to ask great questions that compel them to talk about their problem.

Write down three "go to" questions that you can ask your customers to start a sales conversation.

⭐

....
....
....
....
....
....
....

2. Sell Yourself First

A prospect has to first buy YOU before they buy anything else you have. If you are not willing to promote yourself as a unique brand, with greater value than other sales reps, the customer is done with you after they buy your product. But when the customer buys your brand....your credibility....your expertise, they will continue to buy from you no matter what you sell or what company you work for.

List six qualities that distinguish you from your peers and competitors:
How will you demonstrate these qualities to position yourself as an elite sales pro in your market?

⭐⭐⭐

....
....
....
....
....
....
....
....
....
....
....
....
....

3. Brilliant With The Basics

Unfortunately, it is common for accomplished and experienced salespeople to take their knowledge and skills for granted. There are countless examples of companies and individuals who develop hubris that eventually lead to their downfall. In sales, consistency in sharpening and employing basic skills is the true dividing line between a really good rep and a Superstar. The discipline to be technically sound, while also bringing the full complement of expert knowledge and advanced selling skills into daily sales conversations is what makes a sales professional AMAZING!

Name 3 "basic" selling skills you can use more effectively in your calls:
How can you ensure you will use these skills in every call?

⭐⭐⭐

....
....
....
....
....
....
....
....
....
....
....

4. They're Coachable

Every person who is or was ever considered the best in the world at what they do had a coach. LeBron James, Tom Brady, Muhammad Ali, Steve Jobs, and Oprah all had coaches to help mold and shape them into icons of their industry and it's no different for salespeople. They drive you to levels of performance you could not possibly achieve alone. A coach is there to challenge your thinking and perceived limitations. They don't allow you to believe the hype created by those who admire you. And elite performers crave the candor of a great coach who is not easily enamored with who they are to keep their winning edge.

What type of coaching brings the best out of you?
What type of coaching turns you off?
Who would be an excellent coach for you?

⭐

....

....

....

....

....

....

....

....

....

....

5. Thoroughly Research Every Prospect and Customer

Check your prospect or customer's website and social media profiles for background information on their business and life experiences. A website and company LinkedIn page can reveal both victories and difficulties that need to be addressed. Additionally, social media has information on a customer's hobbies, alma mater, favorite sports team, and even their family. You don't have to discuss it all on one visit, but let your prospect know you've been researching them. Knowing this personal information creates a bond and gives them permission to let their guard down. It may sound like stalking ......and it is, but from a human perspective, a customer appreciates someone taking time to know them rather than just trying to make a sale.

List 12 prospects or customers you will thoroughly research in the next month, and a plan to introduce the information to strengthen your relationship.

⭐

....
....
....
....
....
....
....

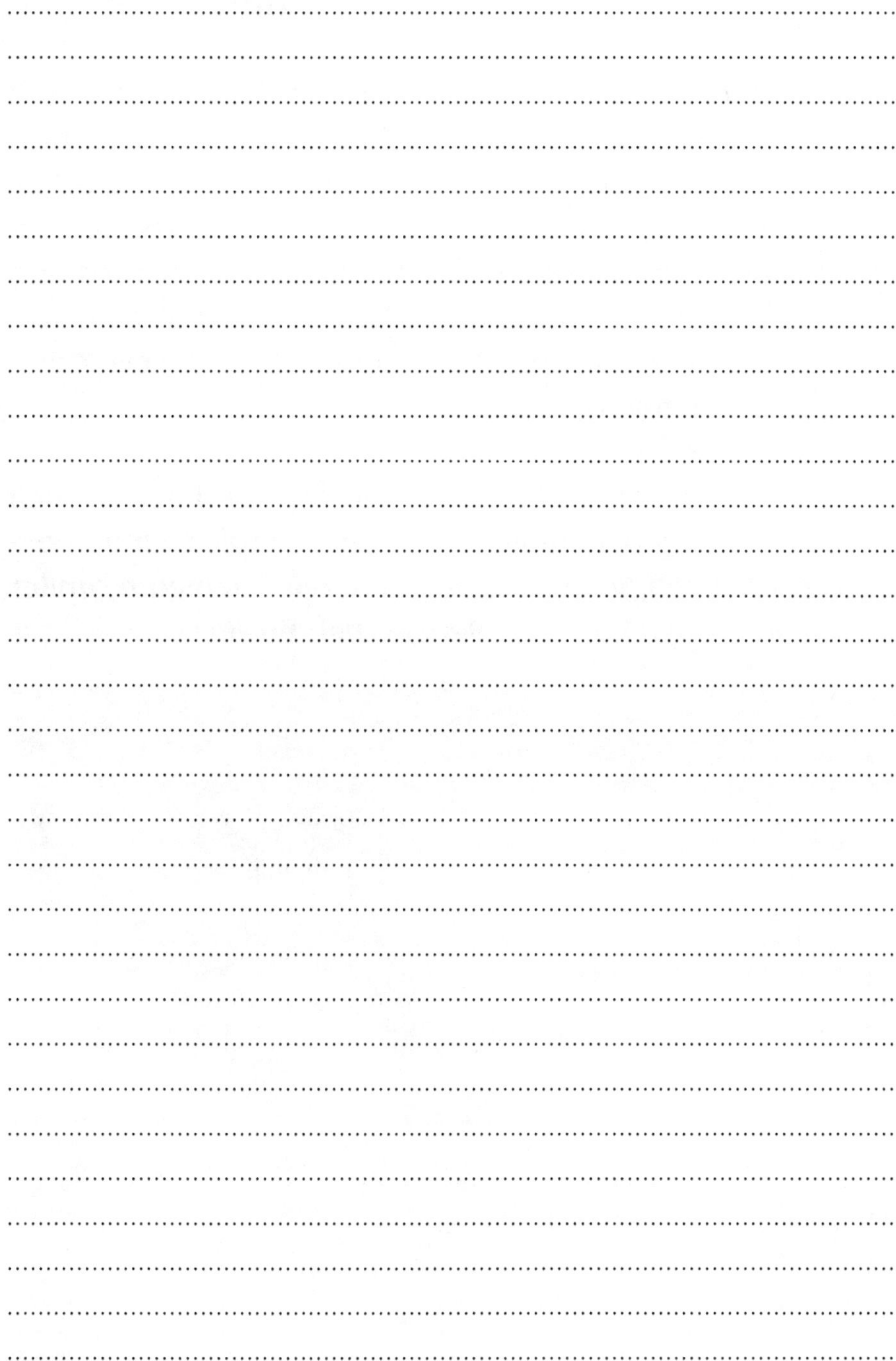

6. Overcome Skepticism With Enthusiasm

Customers decide to buy for emotional reasons and then they justify it with logic. While buyers are skeptical of most salespeople, their skepticism is erased when they see and feel your enthusiasm for what matters to them. A great way to do this is by sharing exciting antidotes and stories from clients that you've helped. Memorable stories delivered with enthusiasm can energize any cynic and put them in a buying mood!

List three difficult objections you face, and match each with an exciting personal story or an example that demonstrates how you, your product, or service helped a similar customer solve a huge problem in their business.

⭐⭐⭐

....
....
....
....
....
....
....
....
....
....
....
....

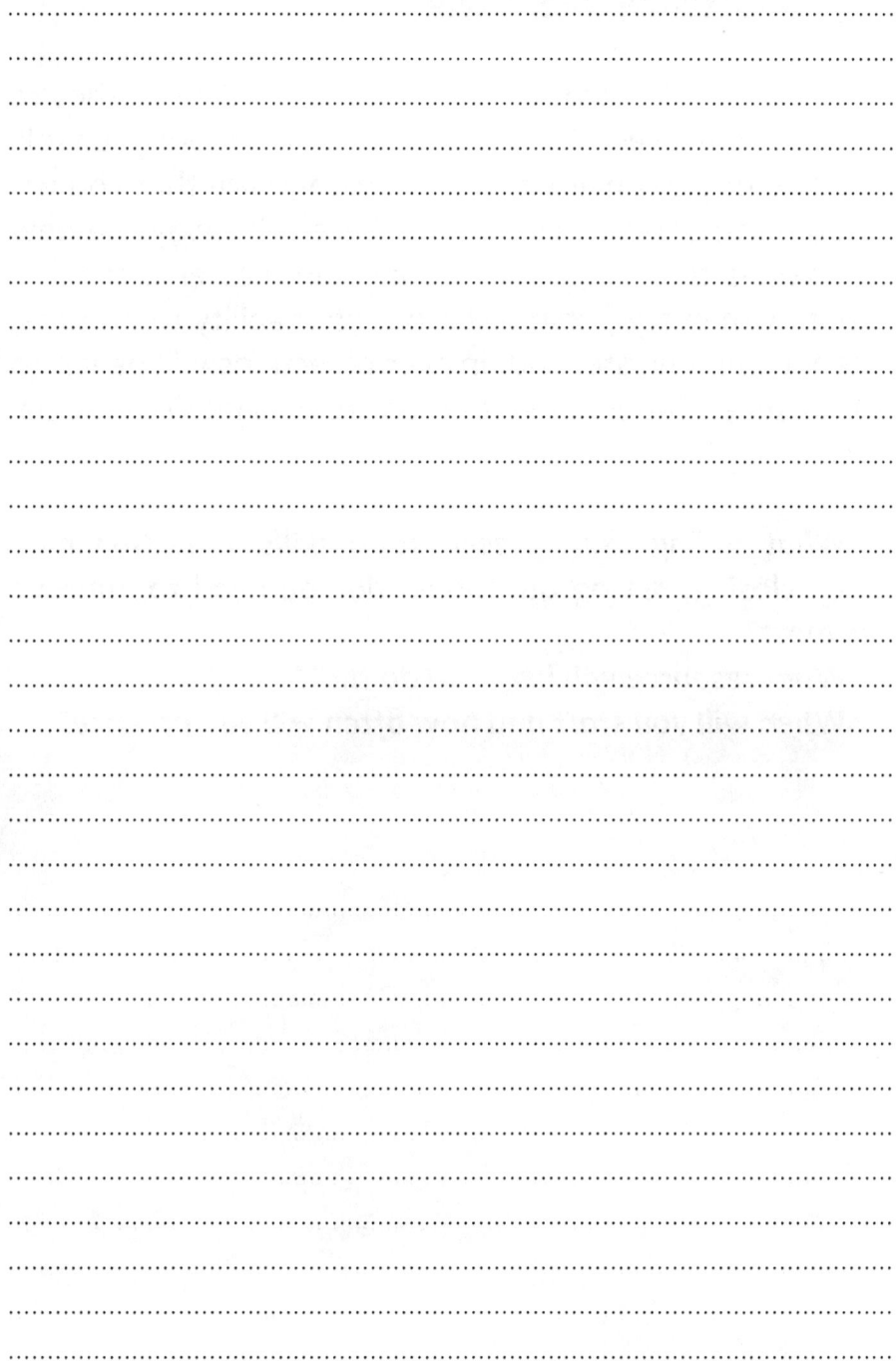

7. Substance Over Style

The best sales pros are not the most polished, they're the most _practiced_. Customers don't care about your selling style or personality type. They only care that you understand their business needs. There will always be new techniques to selling, and no one can master communication with every personality, but your ability to prepare, listen, communicate, and answer objections will never go out of style. Superstar sales pros are brilliant with the basics!

What selling skill (presentation skills, objection handling, closing, asking questions) do you need to improve the most?
What resource will help you do that?
When will you start and how often will you practice?

⭐⭐⭐

....
....
....
....
....
....
....
....
....
....

8. Love Competitive Selling

Although they don't have to do it often, Superstar Sales Pros relish the opportunity to completely and definitively crush the competition in a head-to-head sales comparison. **You should always take pride in knowing your competitors' strengths and weaknesses as good or better than they do.** Combine that by knowing your customers' business so well that for each competitor you are able to speak to why your product's value, positioning, quality, or price offers the best solution for their unique business needs.

Think of your top three competitors and your top three customers. Why is YOUR product service a better solution for these customers? List your top three reasons for each competitor.

⭐

....
....
....
....
....
....
....
....
....
....
....
....

9. Never Deal in Absolutes

A true sales pro is passionate about what is important to them and their organization. But elite reps have the wisdom to understand they don't always have to be right. It doesn't serve you to win a battle (a sale) but lose the war (the customer). Always be flexible in matters that benefit the customer, even if it doesn't benefit you [as long as it's legal, moral and ethical!].

Discipline yourself to be open to other perspectives. Be curious and learn. Regardless of where your information came from, try to be objective and give others a chance to be heard no matter how passionate you feel.

Being open to the opinions of others takes practice.
Write a strategy could you use to discipline yourself for being open to different perspectives?

⭐

....
....
....
....
....
....
....
....
....
....

10. Catch The Client's Vision

Company leaders have a long-term vision for their business. Your product must be a solution to help them achieve this vision faster and generate more revenue with less effort. An irreplaceable sales rep discusses the vision with business leaders, understands their role in making it happen, and make it known that they will help these leaders see the vision through. They are emotionally vested in the success of the client's business and they celebrate with the team as they reach their goals. With this approach, your business grows along with your client's business because you are a vital part of their continued success.

What is the 1-3 year business vision of your top three accounts?
Who would know this information?
What needs to happen for your product or service fit into that vision?

⭐

....
....
....
....
....
....
....
....
....

11. Leave Great 1st Impressions

The human mind has difficulty changing its perception once a person has made an impression. Superstar sales pros never take this fact for granted, and always make and effort to show up prepared with great energy to make an impact visually, emotionally, and intellectually. An elite performer's reputation will often precede them, which makes the first impression even more important. The Superstar's goal isn't just to make a sale; it's to impact a life! This is why they close first call sales at a much higher rate than others and also maintain trusting relationships with customers who ultimately do not buy. No matter what you do afterward, the first impression will always shape a customer's perception of you and the value you bring.

What feelings do you hope to leave with a prospect after your first encounter?

⭐⭐⭐

....
....
....
....
....
....
....
....
....
....

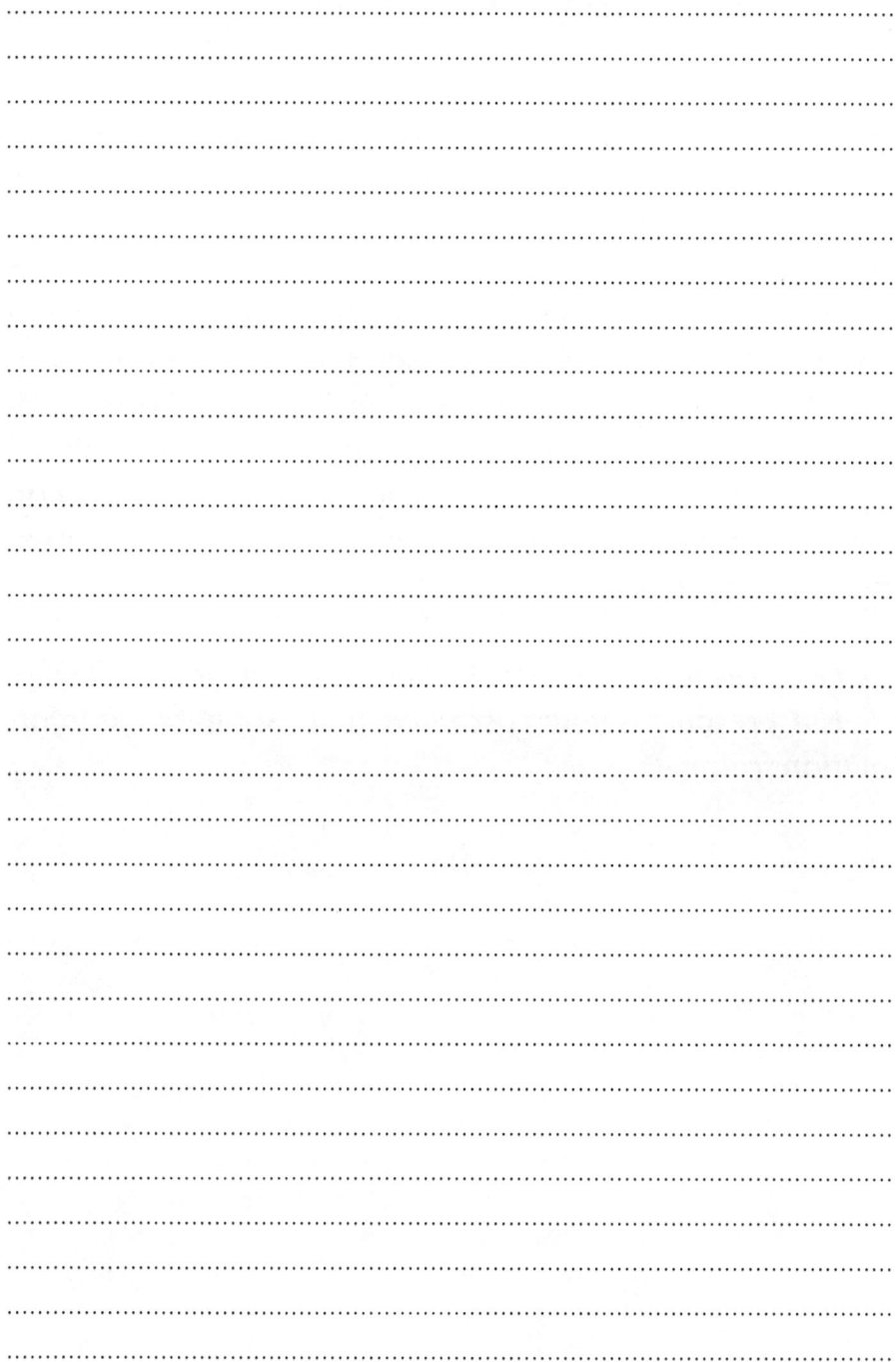

12. Read/Consume Knowledge

With access to information at an all-time high, there's no excuse for being uninformed. Yet so many salespeople are. Leaders are readers! They are a valuable information resource for their clients. Make a habit of following industry thought leaders; read to improve your knowledge and skills; follow discussions in LinkedIn groups. Did you know there is one hour of video uploaded to YouTube every second?? 4 billion videos are viewed each day!! There is a video about virtually anything you want to learn. A disciplined focused effort to consume knowledge daily, especially on a specific topic, can help you become a subject-matter expert in your organization or industry.

List 3 resources that are leading voices of your industry:
List 3 resources your customers follow or get their information from:

⭐

....
....
....
....
....
....
....
....
....
....

13. Public Speaking Skill

The ability to influence and inspire is the highest calling of a leader. Superstar sales performers relish the opportunity to present to larger audiences. A memorable presentation or speech leaves the lasting impression of a strong leader on your customers. You don't have to be the smartest person in the room. The person talking in front of the room is the perceived expert because that's what people will remember. Consensus and acceptance of your presentation will endear you to an organization. If you can win over a room of people, you can win a contract!

List three opportunities do you have to improve your public speaking skills?

⭐⭐⭐

....
....
....
....
....
....
....
....
....
....
....
....

14. Poise

Superstar sales pros don't allow customers to intimidate them. They do not feel pressure to make decisions or commitments to a customer just to make a sale. Superstars know it takes time to truly understand a customer's business and the unique challenges they face. Making hasty decisions can increase the risk of selling that customer the wrong solution. Plus, without properly qualifying a prospect or customer, you will get beat up on price every time! It takes patience and skill to close and keep big accounts.

Superstars know how to play the game... slow the conversation down ... listen critically and respond intelligently ... stroke the ego of the key influencers ....build relationships for life.

What selling situations would developing greater poise help you?
How can you practice building poise each day?

⭐

....
....
....
....
....
....
....
....

15. Winning Energy

When you show up with confidence and a great attitude, these qualities are attributed to your product or service. To be an elite sales pro, you must be excited about what you do for clients. Even if you're selling widgets, you must believe those widgets are critical to the success of your customer's business, and show them you are excited to be a part of their winning team. Clients are thirsty for that kind of energy and they want to associate themselves with winners.

What are some ways that you can prepare yourself to show up with enthusiasm and confidence for your next appointment?

....

....

....

....

....

....

....

....

....

....

....

....

....

....

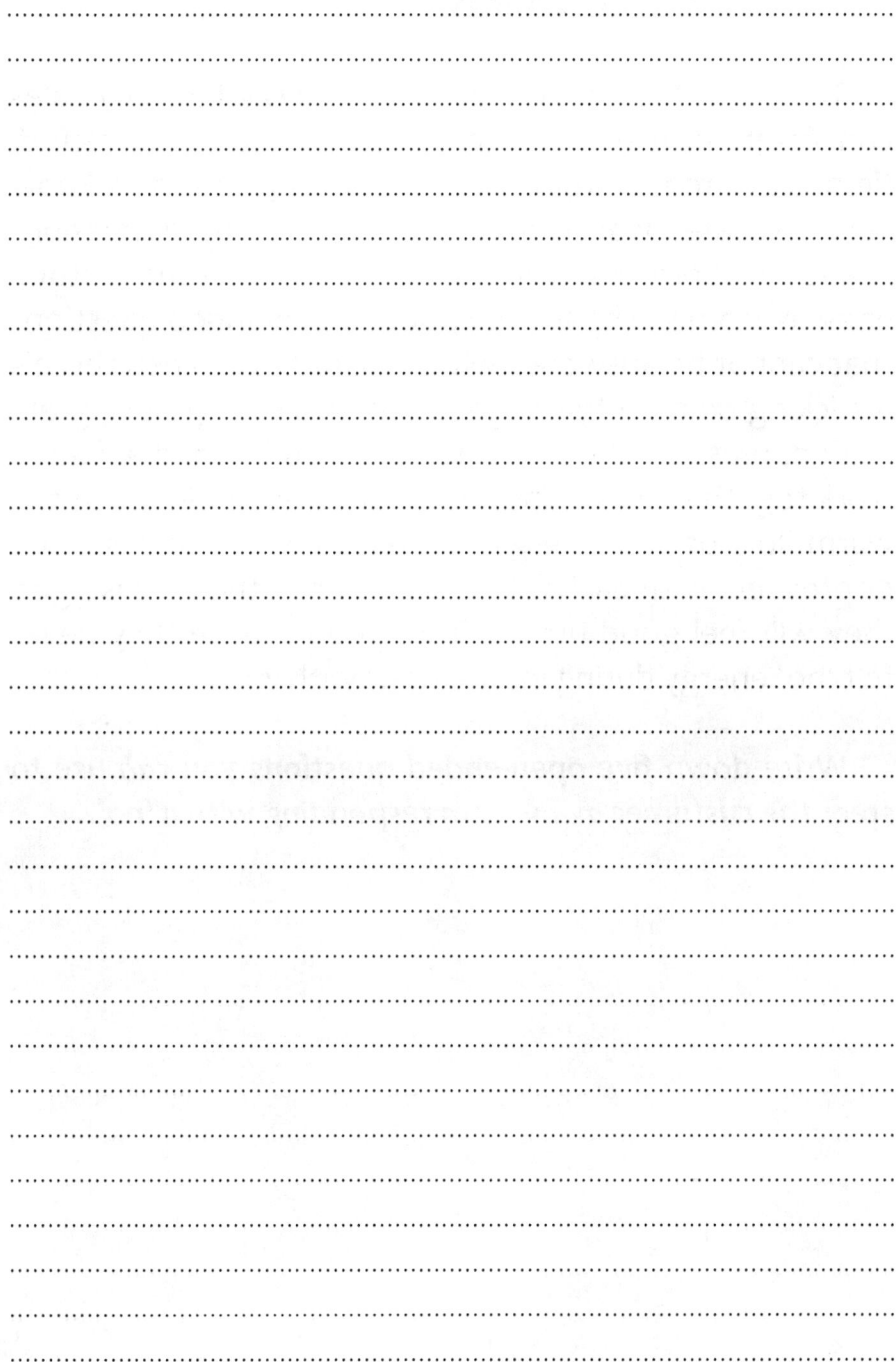

16. Avoid "No" Energy

The word 'no' infuses negative energy into any sales conversation. It suggests rejection and finality and can stifle positive momentum. But, elite sales performers know how to create a warm atmosphere that promotes possibility and collaboration. They know how to steer the customer away from saying 'no' by asking open-ended questions that cannot be answered with 'yes' or 'no'. When there's a sticking point in the negotiation or a strong buying objection, reassure the customer that you will find a way to work together. It may not be at the present time, but the warm flow of 'yes' energy will remain with that customer or prospect with each future visit. When the time is right, they will feel good buying from you because they never felt 'no' energy during interactions with you.

Write down five open-ended questions you can use to steer the customer away from responding with a 'no'.

⭐

....
....
....
....
....
....
....
....
....

17. Mirror The Customer's Energy

Superstar Sales Pros are masters at reading and projecting non-verbal communication. This is a very subtle technique in which you mirror the other person's posture and body movements. Studies show that mirroring makes a person feel more familiar and comfortable with you. However, if the customer has negative energy or closed body language, a skilled rep is mindful and careful not to be influenced by their disposition. Instead, they inject life into the conversation through their voice and project more open body language to make a connection that builds trust and rapport.

Before each call make a mental note to take notice of the customer's mood and body language.

Make a conscious effort to either mirror positive energy and motion, or project more positive energy and body language into the conversation.

Record your observations daily and notice how long it take for it to become instinctual.

⭐⭐⭐

....
....
....
....
....
....
....

18. Preparation

The key to performance excellence is preparation. Every sales call presents an opportunity to demonstrate excellence, no matter how mundane it may seem. The best sales professionals plan an objective for each call and anticipate the many directions the conversation may go. Obsessive preparation for a customer's needs wants, objections, complaints, technical questions or loyalty to your competition shows you are a polished subject matter expert that will be an asset to their business.

What area of product or industry knowledge do you need to improve?
What measurable difference would it make in your daily sales conversations?

★★★

....
....
....
....
....
....
....
....
....
....
....

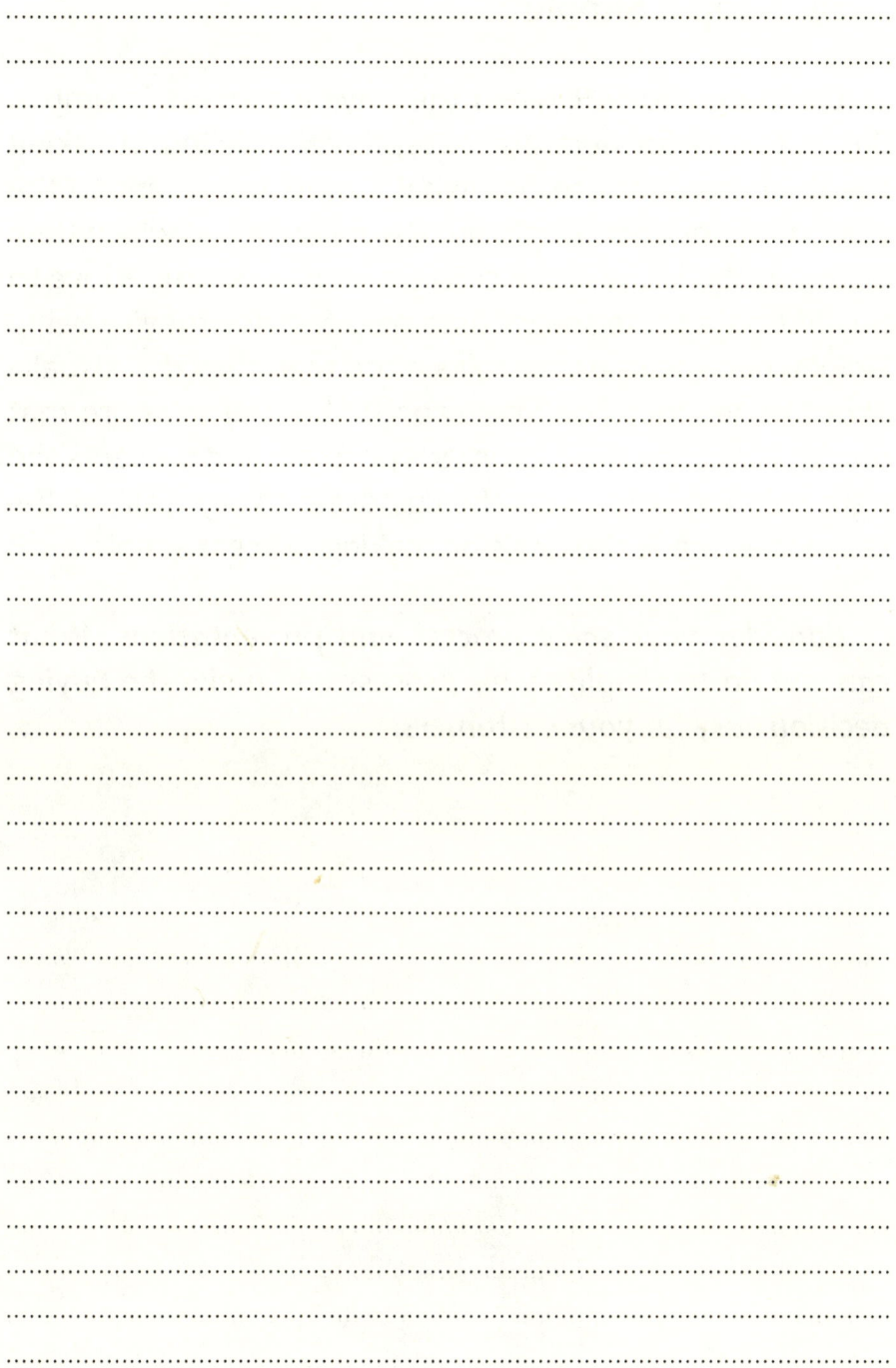

19. Keep It Simple

Customers love it when the buying process is simple. Superstar performers are exceptionally skilled in asking the right questions to find what's most important to the customer, and then single out the must-haves, which then becomes the focus of the conversation. Customers love to buy but hate to be sold. Customers feel like they're being 'sold' when the sales rep talks more than they do. Usually about things they don't care about. But the sales pro that quickly identifies the customer's problem and presents the right solution empowers the customer to say 'yes', all because they made the decision making process simple.

Consider your sales process and presentations. What can you do to simplify your process and make the buying decision easy for your customers?

⭐⭐⭐

....
....
....
....
....
....
....
....
....
....

20. Timing

As with most things in life... timing is everything. Great timing in sales means staying in tune with account buying cycles, budget renewals, proposal opportunities, personnel changes, and competitive intelligence. Average performers strike gold every now and then, but superstars are intentional with timing. They make contact with the right people throughout the year to strengthen their relationship and capture the vision of the customer's organization. When opportunities arise to submit bids or presentations, they have created momentum and relationship equity that the competition cannot compete with.

How many touches will it take to close your next large account?
Who are the most significant individuals you need a relationship to close the sale?

⭐

....

....

....

....

....

....

....

....

21. Do What Others Won't, To Have What Others Don't

Superstar Sales Pros look for opportunities to do the dirty work. Whether crunching numbers, working late hours with and/or for the client, or being the sounding board for a demanding and intimidating client, superstars enjoy the challenge. They do what no one else has the courage or will to do (as long as it's legal, moral and ethical) if they feel the long-term ROI is worth it. Elite reps can have a big ego, but they exhibit no ego problem when it comes to getting and keeping customers.

List the customers whom you feel are worth the effort to wear down with service and thoughtfulness until you can reel them in?

⭐

....
....
....
....
....
....
....
....
....
....
....

22. Quickly Establish A Common Bond

This is the reason warm leads close at a higher rate: the product and/or salesperson is associated with something or someone that the buyer already respects. In the absence of a warm lead, pay attention to the prospect's environment for clues to what you both value and respect. Bring it up in conversation to quickly establish a common bond and create positive vibes. This raises your likability factor immediately!

List 10 customers and the things that you both might share as a common bond:

⭐

....

....

....

....

....

....

....

....

....

....

....

....

....

....

23. Befriend The Gatekeeper

In some situations, the gatekeeper is more important than the actual buyer. Overlook or underestimate this person and your name is mud to that account forever, even if you switch companies. Superstar Sales Pros know the gatekeeper controls access and is a vital source of intel. They give the same level of respect and interest to the gatekeeper as they do the decision maker. When the gatekeeper is your friend, they protect you from competitive threats, give you ideas to be more successful, and can be your voice when you're not around.

How much do you know about the gatekeeper in your most difficult to sell targets?

What do you want them to know about you (not your product)?

⭐⭐⭐

....
....
....
....
....
....
....
....
....
....
....

24. Avoid The Gatekeeper

Sometimes befriending the gatekeeper is difficult. In these cases, your best bet is to avoid them. So, what do you do if the gatekeeper's loyalties lie with your competition? Show up early before they're at their post, or later in the day when they've gone home. Most leaders work longer hours than the support staff and are often at the office early in the morning, or long after the close. You can also find days or times when someone else is gate keeping and befriend them to gain access. Savvy sales pros are attentive to the habits and hobbies of potential clients: Where do they park? What time do they have lunch? Do they leave or eat in the office? What do they like to do outside the office? Who can introduce you? To be an elite sales pro the gatekeeper can never be an obstacle.

List three of your toughest sales targets to access, and for each, list three actions you will take to get in front of them.

⭐

....
....
....
....
....
....
....
....

25. Look For Disaster

Customer disaster or panic provides the perfect opportunity for a sales professional to be a hero. With a little creativity, flexibility and quick thinking, you can single-handedly save a customer's day, month or year! This works especially well on customers you have been unable to close. Send them seasonal reminders to call you in a pinch, or for a business emergency that their current vendor cannot handle. If you offer... make sure you're ready to shine when it happens! It's an open door to calm an otherwise chaotic situation. You will win favor and gratitude and may even land the account by simply being attentive.

What are common disasters your customers experience, and how can you help if given the opportunity?

⭐

....
....
....
....
....
....
....
....
....
....
....

26. Sale or No Sale....Follow-Up

One big difference between the Superstar and the mid-level sales performer is what happens when they don't make the sale. The mid-level performer says "good-riddance!" However, the Superstar follows-up with as much detail and gratitude as they would with a customer who placed a big order. Things change: business needs change; opinions of your product change. But what does not change is the impression you leave with prospects you encounter. Showing class and appreciation after being told 'no' lets the customer know the kind of experience they could have with you as a business partner now or in the future. Superstars know follow-up leads to a fortune in all circumstances.

List 12 accounts you need to follow-up with, and the most strategic way to contact them in order to start the dialogue:

★★★

....
....
....
....
....
....
....
....
....

27. Be An Interesting Person

A common trait of highly successful sales professionals is that they are truly fascinating people. They have cool hobbies, enjoy thrilling adventures, can tell spellbinding stories, and are an endless source of cultural literacy. It's not so much a gregarious spirit or big personality, but a magnetic quality that draws people to them. In addition to superior skill and product knowledge, they leave the room with greater positive energy than when they entered the room. And they enjoy the kind of relationships and access other reps dream of having with their customers.

How many ways can you make a connection with clients and support staff beyond your product?

⋆⋆⋆

....
....
....
....
....
....
....
....
....
....
....
....
....

28. Industry Ambassadors

Instead of a sole focus on closing deals or being on top of the stack rankings, Superstar Sales Pros take a different approach to their business. They keep up with industry trends, competition, and key opinion leaders, and they share the knowledge liberally with busy clients who have too much on their plate to keep up. They become Wikipedia for the most common problems their customers encounter and the different strategies (good or bad) those customers and other companies in the industry have used to solve them.

Name six industry blogs, journals, website newsletters or experts you can follow to become a greater resource to clients and peers.

✦✦✦

....

....

....

....

....

....

....

....

....

....

....

....

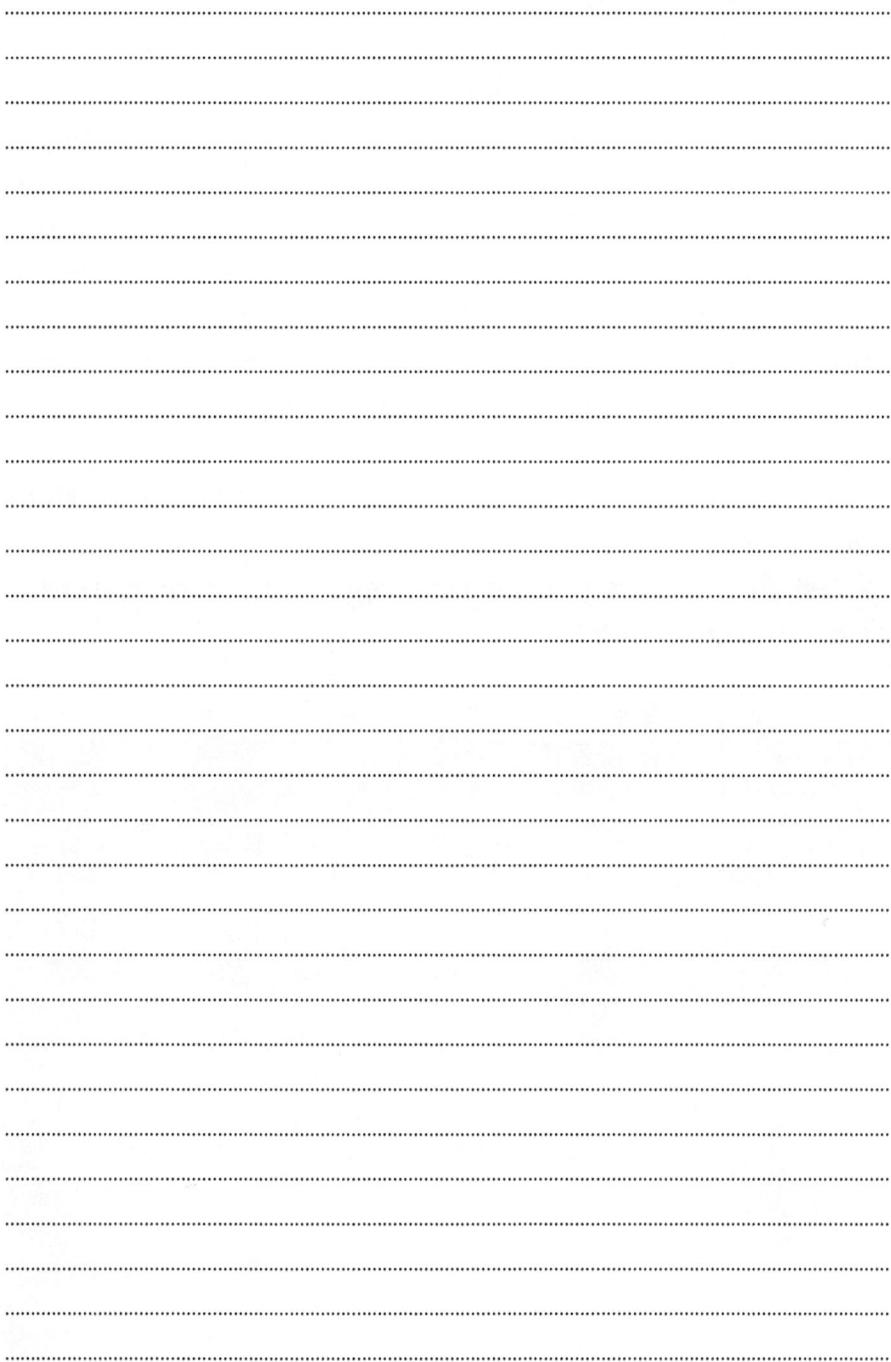

29. Purposeful Communication

There's the art of small talk…and then there's a sales-person who just won't shut up! If you do all the talking you become annoying. Period. Purposeful communication is the key to any great relationship, and it's no different in sales. Engage others by sharing interesting stories. Ask great questions. Provide useful data and information about your product. Be memorable when you're with them and make them miss you when you're gone!

If a customer finds their phone more interesting than you, you're a lot less likely to make a sale.
List five actions you do take regain the attention of a distracted customer?

⭐⭐⭐

....

....

....

....

....

....

....

....

....

....

....

....

....

....

30. Believe Anything Is Possible

In any business negotiation, it is not unusual for customers to make unreasonable demands, but it's simply a starting point to find common ground. When customers ask for something you typically cannot accommodate, present them with a few other options and put the ball back in their court. On the extreme end, let them know what they're asking for could happen, but it would take an equally unusual commitment from them to come close. Whether long-term agreements, volume requirements, or co-branding opportunities, take advantage of these moments to expand your idea of what's possible with your clients. Given the proper perspective, it is possible to create win-win situations with even the most demanding customers when you think anything is possible.

List one example from your experience where a customer made an unreasonable demand. Write down one way you could have (or did) take advantage of this opportunity.

⭐

....
....
....
....
....
....
....
....

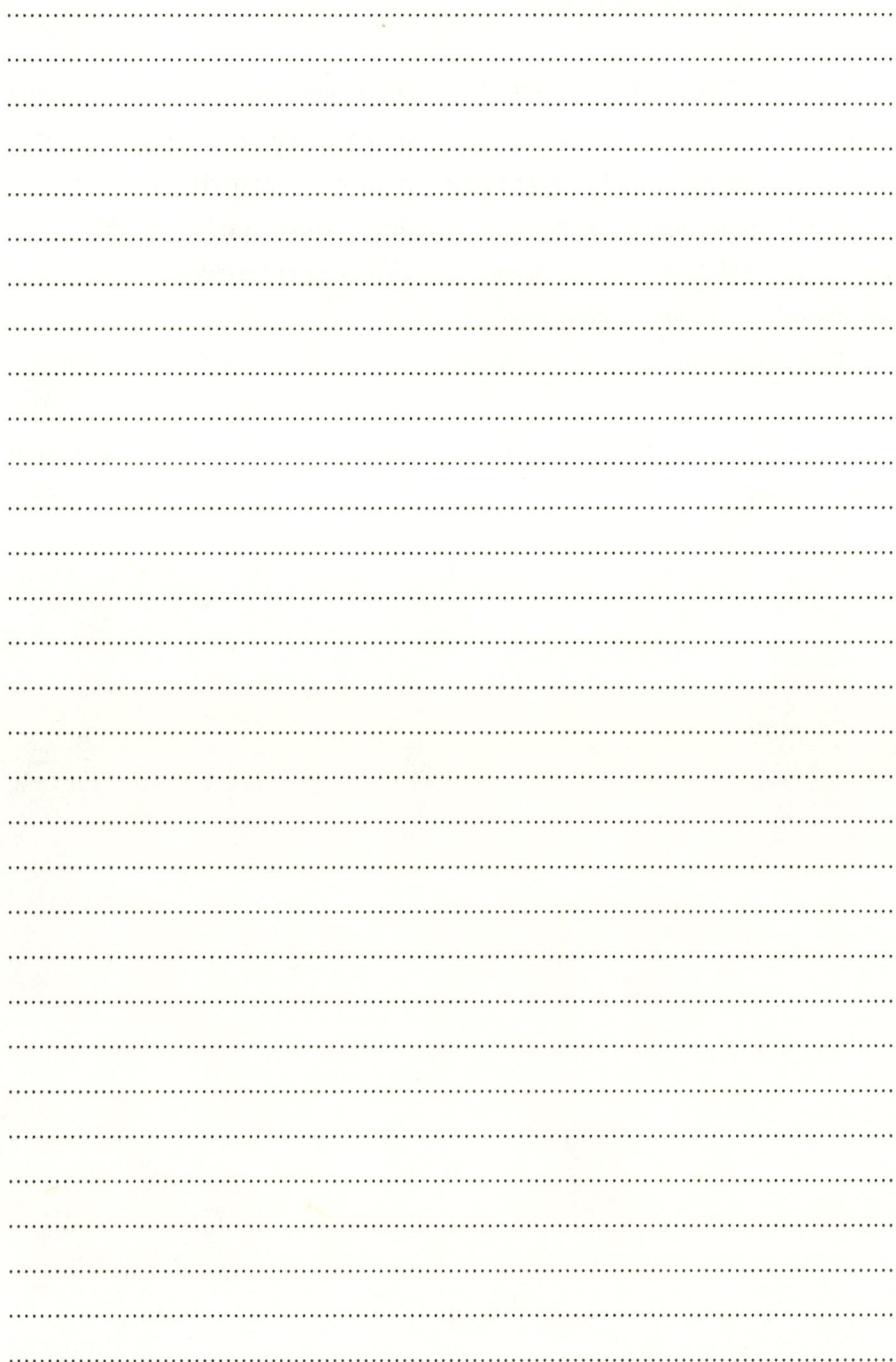

31. Stay Informed

Stay informed about things that are happening around you- in your industry –your community, current events, how the local sports teams are doing ….anything that you can pull and weave into a conversation with people. Superstars take current news and use it to make a case for increasing their business.

For example:

What are hot topics in your industry that affect buying decisions?

⭐⭐⭐

....
....
....
....
....
....
....
....
....
....
....
....
....
....
....

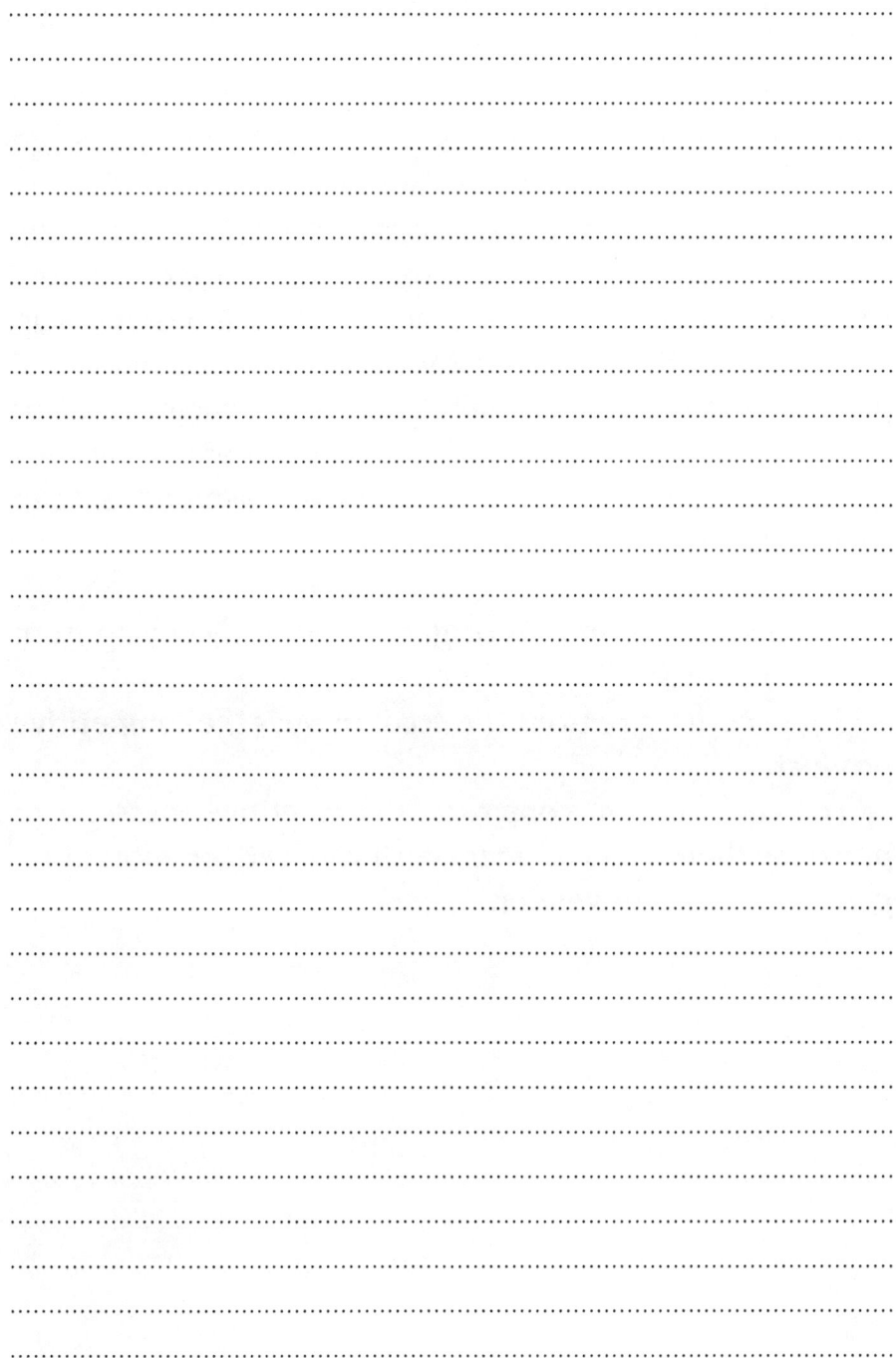

32. Study The Competition

At least once a year you should update your knowledge of competing products. How does their message position them in the market? Evaluate what's working for these businesses in the areas of marketing, sales strategy, branding, management, and R&D. Stay attuned to how the market feels about your brand and how it measures up to the competition. Superstars know their competitors' product and message as well as they know their own. For every competitor's product, feature, or benefit, great reps know how to turn it into a competitive selling advantage for themselves.

List 6 accounts on your target list currently buying from your competitor.

For each, list 2 reasons the account buys the competitive product.

For each reason, construct a competitive message to persuade them to do business with you, with or without replacing the current vendor.

⭐

....
....
....
....
....
....
....

33. If You Can't Beat Em' ... Join Em'!

No brand can stay on top forever. If you sense the brand you're selling is becoming outdated, or that another brand has entered the market as an innovative and disruptive force, make a power move for yourself! It's a win-win for the Superstar Sales Pro to align their influential personal brand with a perceived innovator or new market leader. New, innovative companies become dominate by putting their products in the hands of salespeople with a "black book" of clients. They tap into your relationship equity to give their brand immediate credibility. It sets the stage for a run of domination built on trust, because clients always want to buy the best product in the market....but most especially from the best rep in the market!

List the clients you can immediately flip if you were to change companies, no questions asked:
List 6 more you would approach but will have questions or reservations:
What will you need to do to convert them?

⭐⭐⭐

....
....
....
....
....
....
....

34. Isolate Objections

Asking open-ended questions gets a prospect talking and keeps them talking about what's most important to them.   Objections surface faster when you attempt to close early and often. With each attempt to close, the real objections or concerns are isolated. This gives you the chance to address them AND ask for a commitment to buy in the same breath. Learning this skill takes the pain and anxiety out of the sales process for your customer - and you will be amazed at how often you close sales on the first call.

Write six strong, open-ended questions for any sales conversation that will compel your customer to be open and transparent about their business needs & concerns:

⭐

....

....

....

....

....

....

....

....

....

....

....

....

35. Don't Let Emotions Get The Best of You

It's human nature to meet aggression with aggression. As tempting as it may be to spar with customers who act like jerks, stay focused on the _buyers need_. Remember, you are there to solve a business problem, not deal with a person who has a problem. If the relationship is mutually rewarding, rake in the commission. If it starts to take away from your quality of life, or the relationship becomes abusive, walk away. Either way, don' t allow your emotions to create undue stress and burn you out. Choose you. Life is too short to deal with assholes!

List 3 customers you've met who have acted like jerks, or have jerk potential:
What's the line a customer would cross to make you walk away?

⭐⭐⭐

....
....
....
....
....
....
....
....
....
....

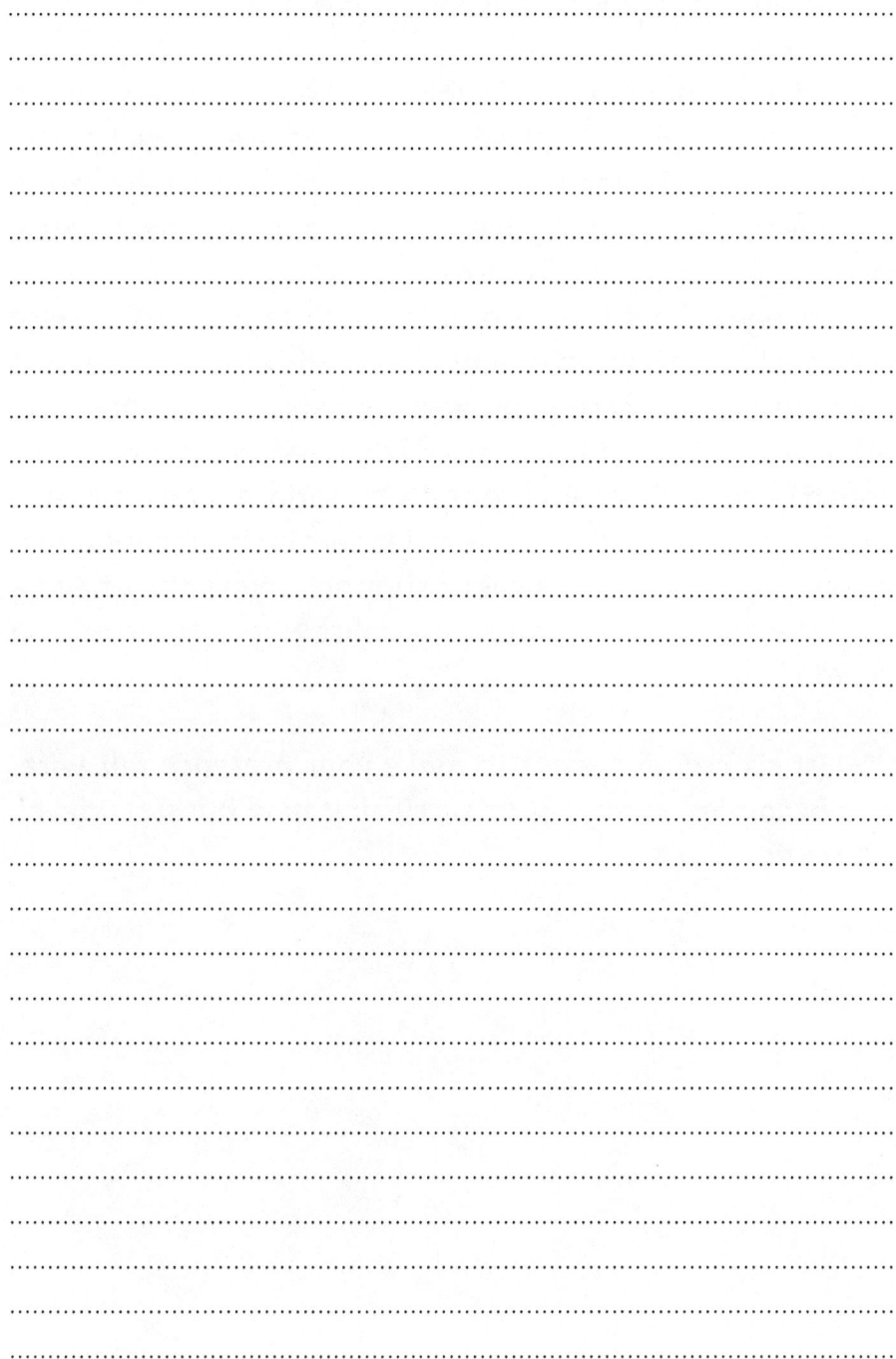

36. Treat Big Fish Like Big Fish

Large accounts or high volume clients are very aware that they are the "Big Fish." They require special attention. When pursuing their business, bring in leaders, product specialist and executives from your company because big fish like to swim with other big fish.

Once you land the account, you don't need to shower personal attention on one or a few individual leaders, but they do expect to see you and they should routinely feel your presence. Treat all issues and needs with a personal touch by returning calls promptly and addressing problems in person. Get the direct line to leaders in the account, and never pass them off to client support unless they have a designated team or account specialist who is an extension of you.

List six creative ways to make your presence felt without becoming annoying or sacrificing new business development:

⭐⭐⭐

....
....
....
....
....
....
....
....

37. Treat All Staff Like VIPs

In a top account, you will most likely see the support staff more than the decision maker or business owner. It only takes a few seconds to make a heartfelt impact on someone's life. A Superstar Sales Pro's presence is felt throughout the organization because they treat everyone in the account like they're a VIP. They show the same sincere energy to target a client, the gatekeeper, the office manager, the new hire, parking attendant, intern, as well as the custodian. They walk the halls of an account like the mayor, knowing a little about each person in the office. Even when the business owner doesn't see the rep, the presence of the Superstar's positive energy is vibrating in the staff long after they visit. That alone makes you a part of the culture, and almost impossible for other vendors to replace.

What's stopping you from becoming the mayor in your accounts?

How can you achieve this level of trust and rapport with your clients?

⭐

....

....

....

....

....

....

38. Feed The Ego

When it comes to spending our hard earned money, we all have big egos. No matter if the purchase is a home, a car or a steak, it's a satisfying experience when someone validates our buying decisions. We need that, . . . even if it is just to feed our ego.

Superstar Sales Pros feed the ego of their buyers in a way that ingratiates themselves to their clients. They express sincere respect and admiration for the client's knowledge and experience, and especially their decision to do business together. Do not patronize, but let the customer know you appreciate learning from them. Some customers need this more than others, but all customers want to feel good about spending their money. Learning to properly feed a buyers' ego can certainly make them feel better about spending their money with you.

List 3 customers with huge egos:
What are the ways you can use to feed their ego in order to build rapport and respect in your relationship?

....
....
....
....
....
....
....

39. Take The Toy Away

Some customers are perfectly willing to make others feel uncomfortable until they get what they want. Telling them 'no' or saying that you can't do something is like teasing a dog with a chew toy. Instead of stoking their aggression with 'no', simply take the toy away. Tell them your product is not the best fit for them. For example, if they want a deeply discounted price, reiterate the quality and suggest that a lesser quality product may better serve their needs. Assure them you are looking out for their best interest. This way you are not rejecting them... .they are making the choice to walk away from something you have clearly positioned as better. These customers do not like it when they can't have what they want, and ultimately, they will tend to do business on your terms.

List three tough customers you can use this technique and write a plan to execute.

⋆⋆⋆

....
....
....
....
....
....
....
....
....

40. Dismiss Price As An Issue

Superstar Sales Pros understand that **price is only an issue if the customer does not clearly see an advantage or the long-term value of their product or service.** The truth is consumers will spend any amount of money to buy exactly what they want....so it's up to you to make them *want* what you're selling. Still, if all things are equal, sell **YOUR** personal value as an asset to their business before negotiating price. If the customer still insists on having a dirt-cheap price that jeopardizes your commission or profitability, walk away. Demanding a lower price is a power play that could set you up for a horrid experience with a customer who does not value you or your product. It's never really about price... it's always about selling value.

List six past customers, whom you did not close, who made price the primary issue for not doing business with you:
Create a strategy to revisit them and reposition the value of your product and personal brand that makes you the only logical choice.

⭐

....
....
....
....
....
....

41. No Emotional Attachment to Rejection

Facing daily rejection is not for the faint of heart. And while high performing sales people have just as many unsuccessful calls as mid-level performers, one decisive reason they ultimately outperform their peers is that they are not emotionally attached to the word "NO". They easily separate rejection of their product or value proposition from the feelings of personal rejection. This allows them to make a higher volume of calls and endure constant rejection with no loss of motivation. Studies have shown over 80% of deals close after 5 follow-ups because trust must be established between the buyer and the vendor. However, more than half of salespeople give up after the first 'NO.' Superstars do not see failure to make the sale as a final verdict; it's only feedback for future sales conversations.

List three follow-up strategies you can use to build trust with your prospects even after they have rejected you.

⋆⋆⋆

....

....

....

....

....

....

....

....

....

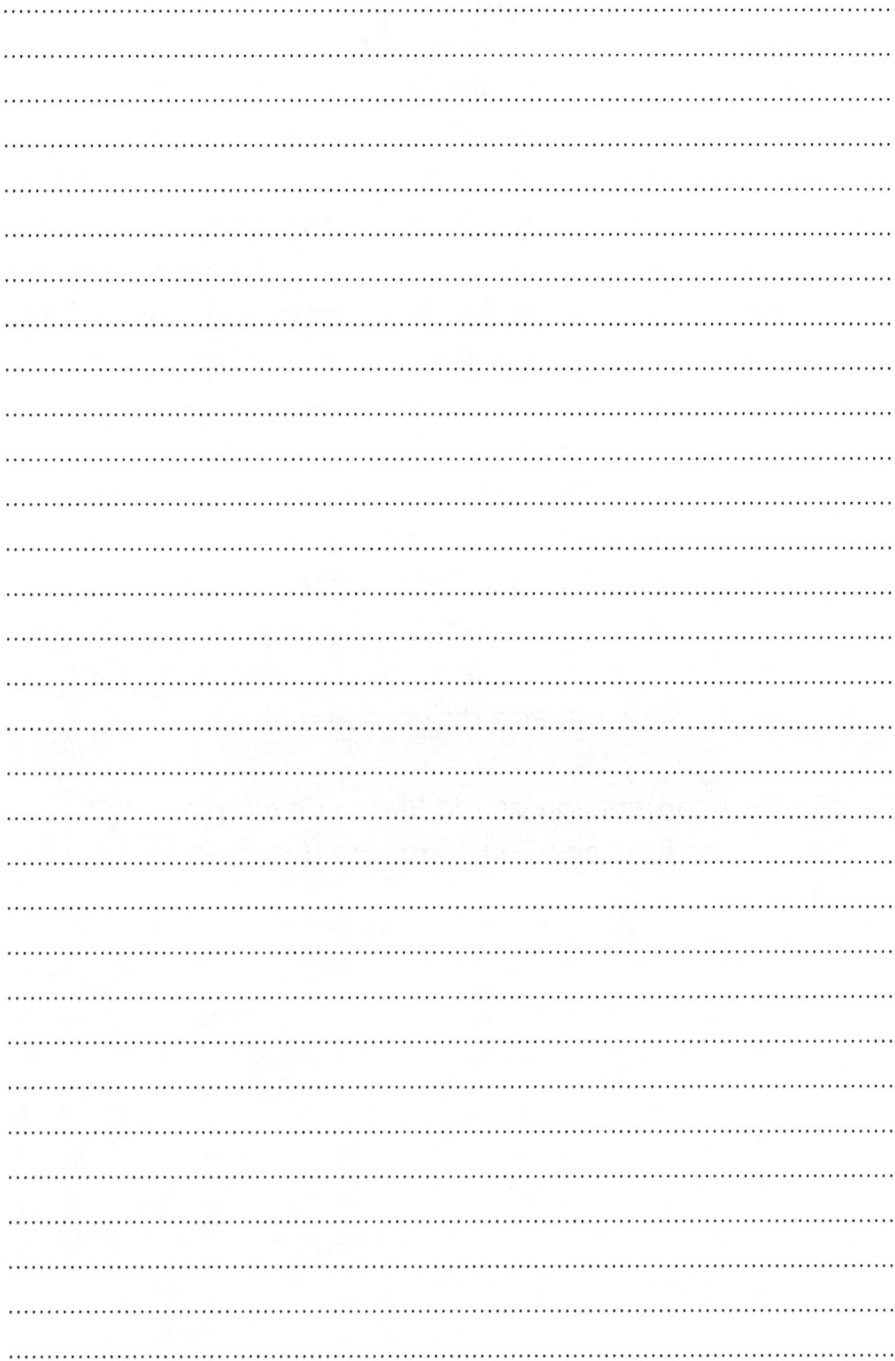

42. Develop Key Opinion Leaders (KOLs)

Salespeople become elite in their industry by turning key customers into evangelists for their personal brand, product or service. Potential KOLs can be found at the local, regional, national and international level of business - whether they buy from you or not. These customers are highly influential among their peers and usually have strong opinions they are willing to share about your business, your competition or the industry. It does not matter if their opinions are good or bad. Leverage their knowledge and bravado by introducing them to executives or product managers at your company to provide valuable customer feedback and market intelligence. It builds your reputation as one who makes things happen, and you gain the trust of powerful people who can champion your message and endorse you as a difference maker.

List 6 customers you would like to develop as a KOL:
What specific area of business can they help you most?

....
....
....
....
....
....
....
....

43. Maintain Relationships After Lost Business

When a customer decides another vendor is a better fit for their business and the business relationship ends, DO NOT let the personal relationship end! You may have lost the business, but the people you worked with in the account will never forget the positive impact you made on their company or them personally. A big decision to switch vendors often has nothing to do with the salesperson, and in time conditions may change in your favor. People who love you get promoted to buying positions or other positions of influence. Or, they may move into other companies and reach out to you again in the future.

List six past customers, buyers, or accounts you enjoyed a good working relationship with, that you can re-engage on a personal level:
What's the best way to reconnect with each of them?

⭐

....

....

....

....

....

....

....

....

....

....

44. Handwritten Thank You Notes

There is one simple reason the practice of handwritten notes is so effective in building long-lasting business relationships: so few professionals even make the effort to write them. This is a standard practice for superstar sales pros. Some even create personalized stationery to further distinguish their professional brand. Even in this era of digital communication, a handwritten note is still a sign of thoughtfulness and class. Great handwritten notes make a profoundly positive impact on the recipient. They are often kept as mementos because clients appreciate the effort, or they're just too good to throw away. Sending the CEO or gatekeeper a professional and sincere handwritten thank you note could even warm the heart of the Grinch who stole Christmas.

List 9 clients, prospects or support staff for whom you would like to express thanks to:

⭐⭐⭐

....
....
....
....
....
....
....
....
....

45. Envision Success

Superstar sales pros experience the day visually before leaving home. They imagine the faces they'll see and the conversations they'll have. They see and hear 'yes' from the first 'hello'! Feeling the energy of success fuels their expectations throughout the day, and they outsell other reps as a result of muscle memory. Visualization is a form of self-actualization....each successful vision simply expands on how they see themselves and what's possible. Because of this, visualization is powerful, because when you expect more, you prepare for more!

Which upcoming presentation can you apply this habit to?

⭐⭐⭐

....
....
....
....
....
....
....
....
....
....
....
....

46. Manufacture Positive Thoughts/Energy

It is critical to feed your mind positive images and information to fortify your conscious and subconscious being against the daily deluge of negative thoughts. Your mind is fertile ground for whatever you plant in it, so make your first thoughts of the day count! Read inspirational messages, speak affirmations and limit negative noise. Planting good seeds will yield positive thoughts, and positive thoughts create positive energy that customers can feel. Remember GI = GO: Garbage in = garbage out…. Or good in = good out.

What can you do to create positive thoughts and energy?
Create a daily routine, that you are willing to stick to, in order to consistently deposit power and motivation in your mind and spirit.

⭐⭐⭐

....

....

....

....

....

....

....

....

....

....

47. Keep Goals In Sight

Elite performers have a system or routine to keep goals in sight. Goal-setting is not goal-getting. Achieving goals is an ongoing process that begins and ends with focus. You must keep your goals in focus. Literally. Billionaire businessman Bill Bartman said he attributes his wealth to reviewing his goals once a day for at least 15min. Awareness is the best way to ensure measurable action each day.

Do you have written goals? [if you answer is no, write them down]

Where do you keep them? [if they're out of sight, they're out of your mind. Try placing them in your phone]

How often do you review them? [set an alarm once a day for you to review them.]

★★★

....
....
....
....
....
....
....
....
....
....
....

48. A Healthy Sense of Self-Worth

Being at top of the stack rankings brings company-wide visibility and can be very stressful because the only place to go is down. The pressure to continue to perform can be overwhelming because, like it or not, many are waiting for that person to fall. But what makes the Superstar at home at #1 is their own self-image and sense of worthiness. They *believe* they are supposed to be #1! This is a self-fulfilling prophecy that motivates them to take more risk and has a profound effect on their ability to negotiate and close sales. Belief in your own self-worth gives you thicker skin to endure constant rejection and minimizes any fear of failure or making mistakes.

List 6 sales goals:
For each goal, list a reason why you __deserve__ it!

★★★

....
....
....
....
....
....
....
....
....
....
....

49. Build A Strong Professional Brand

When your name is consistently on top of the stack rankings, you become a brand people want to be associated with. And the reason Superstar performers stay on top, is the tremendous respect clients have for them. This hard-earned relationship equity is at the core of a strong professional brand because your brand influence comes from what people say about you after you leave the room. When customers experience competent and credible professionals who add value to their business, they gladly refer you to members of their network because they trust you.

Remember, customers, buy **you**, before they buy anything else you're selling. Superstars double the closing rate of the mid-level performer by attracting customers with a reputation that precedes them.

Name five elements you want to be associated with your brand (e.g.-trust, cool, trendy, exclusive, experienced, etc):
How can you build your brand reputation through your digital imprint as well as through personal interaction?

⭐⭐⭐

....
....
....
....
....
....

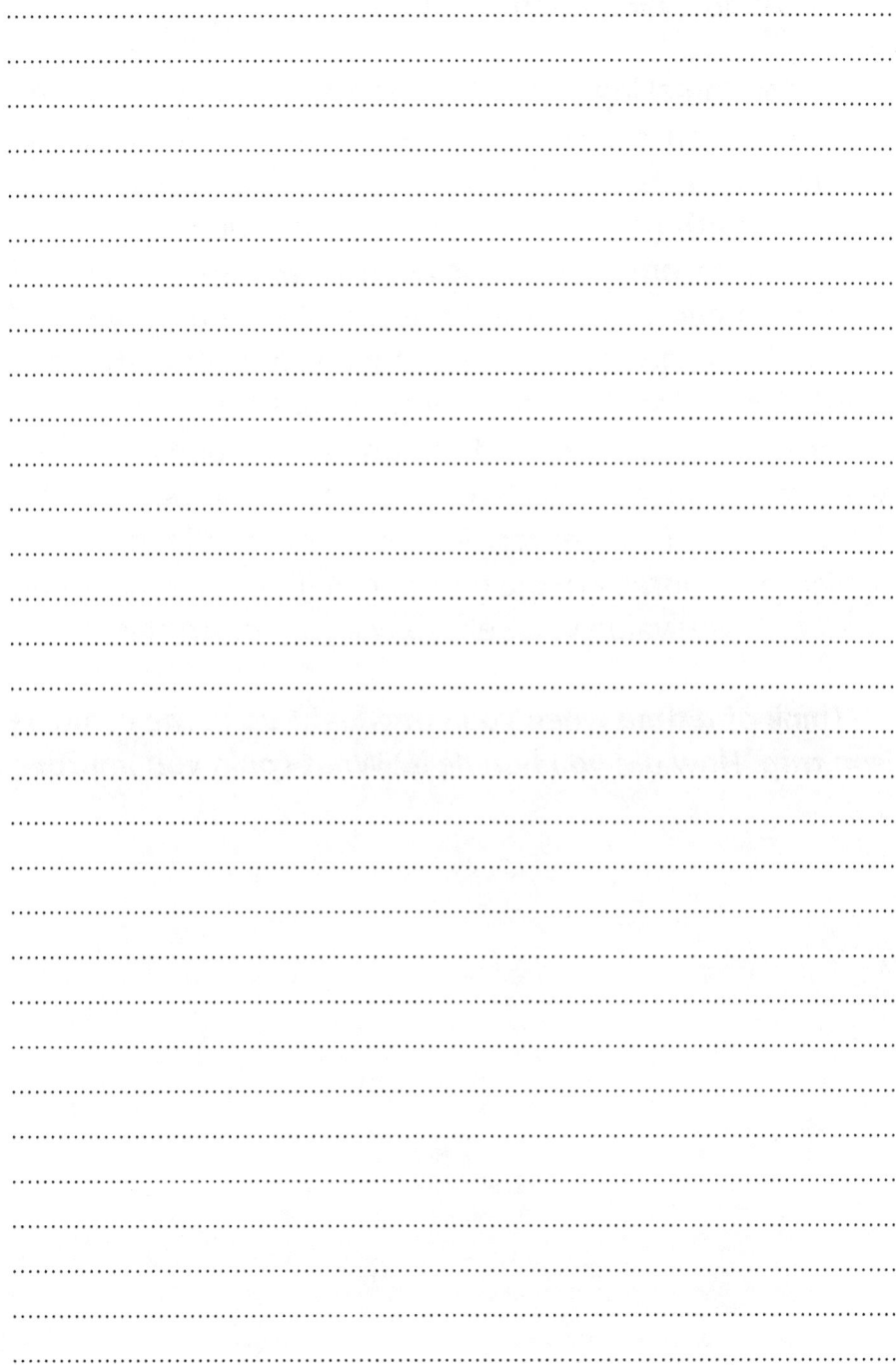

50. Avoid The Trap of Comparison

Although selling is a profession fundamentally based on comparison, the Superstar Sales Pro's sole focus is how to improve in order to exceed their own goals. Being pre-occupied with how you measure up to others takes your focus away from understanding who you are today, and who you need to become to accomplish your goals. All competitors should be aware of what the competition is doing. Learn from the competition; take innovative ideas and make them your own. But don't allow yourself to lose sight of the unique challenges of your business and the solutions you must deliver. Most importantly, learn to recognize and appreciate the gifts and abilities that make you unique. If you value yourself, so will your customers.

Think of a time when you got caught up in the comparison trap. How did you handle it? What could you improve on?

⭐⭐⭐

....
....
....
....
....
....
....
....
....

51. Well Networked/Connectors

Superstars create distinct networks with former co-workers, college friends, industry contacts and clients with the goal of adding value to the people in those networks. Networking is not "gimmie all you can gimmie!" It's more about what you can do, and have done for others that make you a valuable member of their network. When you find out a person has something in common with another professional in your network, make a connection. They appreciate the opportunity to expand their network and immediately see you as a valuable professional resource they need to stay close to.

List 3 sources from which you can create distinct professional networks:
Write a list of names with whom you are most familiar with from these different settings that constitute your value network:

⋆★⋆

....
....
....
....
....
....
....
....
....

52. Maintain A Healthy Pipeline

Although the Pareto Principle is true in business, commonly known as the 80/20 Rule (80% of results come from 20% of customers; therefore 80% of a sale reps time should be devoted to them), Superstar Sales Pros are very intentional about nurturing the 80%. They are the best opportunities for sales growth in your pipeline.

Even though you may not see these customers as often, deliberately deliver excellence when you do see them to adequately qualify their potential and business needs. As seasons change, so do the needs and personnel of your customers.   According to Genius.com, 66% of buyers reported that consistent and relevant communication from the company was the key influence to buy from that company. It only takes one time for the current vendor to slip up. Or one turnover of a key decision maker for your breakthrough opportunity to close a major account to present itself.

Identify 8 accounts currently qualified as B or C-level priorities:
Create a lead nurturing plan to move these accounts through your pipeline, touching them at least once/month for one year. Measure your progress (sales increase, better relationships, market intel) each quarter during the year before you decided to cut them from the plan.

★★★

53. Never Satisfied

Superstar sales pros have an innate drive that compels them to do their best. This is often perceived as a gift and a curse, because no matter how outstanding the accomplishment, they never seem to be satisfied. The more they achieve, the desire to achieve even higher goals grows in order to maintain their own self-image. Superstars are their own worst critics, and in some cases, are uncomfortable receiving compliments and find it difficult to enjoy the success they have earned. Being a superstar is not all fun and games. It comes with a price that few are willing to pay.

After a great sales achievement, how do you stay motivated to reproduce or top it?

★★★

....

....

....

....

....

....

....

....

....

....

....

54. Practice The Law of Sowing & Reaping

This is the secret to superstar success in selling: you reap what you sow. Your seed is your prospecting effort, articulating your value proposition, asking thought-provoking questions, leaving marketing collateral, and providing expert insight to solve your customers' problem. Your seeds must be of excellent quality to bear good fruit, but every seed you plant won't grow and the seeds that do will produce varied results. Superstar reps know they cannot control what a given account produces, but the reason they out produce their peers each year is they *consistently* plant a greater number of seeds.

In your industry, what is the planting season (slow business period) vs. the harvest season (peak season)?

How are your efforts to develop new business affected in each season?

How can you maintain efforts to build new business during peak seasons?

⭐

....

....

....

....

....

....

....

More products from Rome Madison

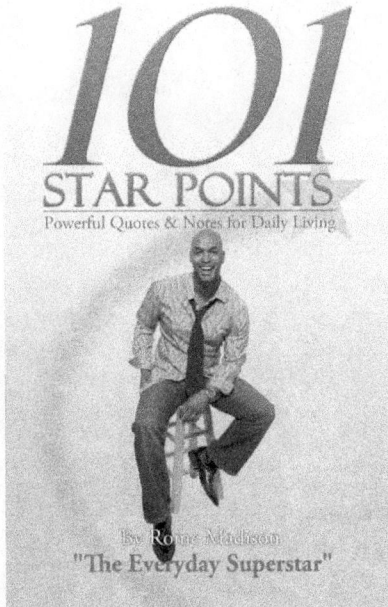

Find these works and much more at www.RomeMadison.com

The Superstar Academy

THE FIGHT OF YOUR LIFE!

Rome helps leaders and sales teams to

FIGHT! ....COMPLACENCY.

Complacency is the biggest opponent you must fight as a professional. If you fall victim to complacency your product, service or talent will become a commodity in the marketplace. Commoditization or non-diferentiation of your brand is the kiss of death.

In this 50min keynote Rome explains what is required of leadership and indivual contributors to fight for higher goals, increased revenue and winning the title of market leader in your industry.

You will learn:

- Why all forces in the market want you to become a commodity.
- The antidote to complacency and commoditization.
- 3 key disciplines of all innovative leaders and companies.
- How to create an innovative culture that spawns competition and accountability.

LEAD THROUGH INNOVATION: HOW TO WIN IN AN ERA OF FIERCE COMPETITION & RAPID CHANGE

Achieving and maintaining performance excellence isn't easy or comfortable. It's Hard!

So why do some companies and teams make it look so easy while others struggle to separate from the pack? Drawing from his 20-year career of commercializing cutting edge technologies and lessons learned from perennial winning teams, Rome teaches the four dominant qualities of Innovative Leaders and why they consistently outperform the competition.

In this 50 min keynote you will learn:

- How to think like a 1%'er.
- How curiosity spawns creativity in an organization.
- How to be brutal honesty, but not brutal to affect change.
- How to create a sense of purpose to champion change in your organization.

WINNING INFLUENCE: HOW TO LEAD WITHOUT THE TITLE

There's a big difference between management and leadership. Most employees will follow you if a paycheck depends on it, but developing leadership skills to influence others helps you build a professional brand that will pay residual dividends in your career regardless of title or position.

This presentation is excellent for team building activity or breakouts (3-4hrs). It can also be delivered as a keynote presentation.

You will learn:

- The importance of your professional brand.
- How to gain permission from others to lead them.
- How to demonstrate leadership capacity among peers and as a young professional.
- How to create momentum that gets you noticed by leaders & executives.
- How to ace the ultimate test of leadership before being hired or promoted.

THE SUPERSTAR SALES ACADEMY: 7 HABITS OF TOP 10%'ERS

There's a reason top sales performers stay at the top, while the majority are inconsistent mid-level performers. It's less about talent and ability; it's about skill development and daily habits!

A few of the habits include:

- Self Mastery
- Critical Thinking
- Focus on Big Results & Big Money
- Listening for 'Yes'
- Much, much more!

This is a half-to-full day sales workshop to help your team actively incorporate the skills and habits of elite Superstar Sales Professionals. This is an interactive session that uses improv, competition and the creativity of your team to inspire growth and set bigger goals.

Even award-winning sales reps need to improve. They demand and expect the best to help them grow and Rome Madison is a voice elite sales professionals recognize and follow!

WWW.ROMEMADISON.COM

BOOK ROME NOW ▶

The Superst★r Academy

CORPORATE ENGAGEMENT PROGRAMS

EXECUTIVE COACHING

Rome is ICF certified through the Coach Diversity Institute. Its critical for organizations to help executives and high-potential employees prepare for rapid societal change happening today. Rome's rich experience as an executive, and his coaching skill will help your leaders gain self-awareness, clarify goals, achieve developmental objectives faster, and increase their value as a diversity and leadership professional.

SEE ROME IN ACTON

The Superstar Academy   Winning Influence   Keynote Speaker

ROME'S PARTIAL CLIENT LIST

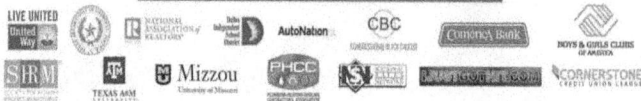

Book Rome For - Conference Keynote or Breakout Speaker, National Sales Meetings, Team Building, Millennial Leadership Development, Black History Month.

SPEAKER REQUIREMENTS

- ✓ LCD Projector & Screen
- ✓ FlipChart with Paper & Markers (For audiences of less than 100)
- ✓ A Wireless Lavaliere Mic
- ✓ 1/8 Audio Input Jack (Headphone Jack) so Rome can patch into House Sound
- ✓ 6-Foot Skirted Product Table placed in High-Traffic Area

• Rome's Success Store: Maximize Your Potential, Own Your Power and **FIGHT FOR MORE!**

WWW.ROMEMADISON.COM

BOOK ROME NOW ▶

www.ingramcontent.com/pod-product-compliance
Lightning Source LLC
Chambersburg PA
CBHW022058190326
41519CB00036B/682